Y0-DNN-255

Praise for Loving Outside the Lines

"When you read *Loving Outside the Lines,* you'll feel again how love rules all and how living with an open heart is its own kind of genius. This book is a journey of the heart—Jannirose's, Charlie's and yours."

LYNNET MCKENZIE, CO-AUTHOR OF
LIVING A JOYFUL, JUICY LIFE

"We feel like our hearts have been cracked wide open. For us, *Loving Outside the Lines* has been an introduction to a teacher in the truest, deepest, most Divine sense of the word. This is a book worth carrying with you everywhere you go."

REV. SANDRA ANNE DALY, AUTHOR OF *CHOOSE YOUR UNIVERSE*
RICK DALY, "HAPPY DANCING MAN" AND STILT ENTERTAINER

"In *Loving Outside the Lines*, Jannirose introduces us to her beautiful son Charlie, a boy with a gift for interpreting what we all feel. Charlie—who was born with a hole in his heart—is able to reach through our inner clutter and pull at our heart-strings, while Jannirose points us to a happier tomorrow through Charlie's poignant teachings."

DR. LOREN WOLD, CHAIR OF MEDICAL ADVISORY BOARD,
SAVING TINY HEARTS SOCIETY

Loving

Outside the Lines

Blessed are the pure in heart,
for they shall see God.

MATT.5:8

Loving

Outside the Lines

Lessons From an Earth Angel

Jannirose JOY Fenimore

Special Prayers by Charlie Fenimore

Author of *Happy in Soul*

Cover design © by Gaelyn Larrick
Cover photograph © by Andrea Chapelo
Interior design by Christy Collins, C Book Services

Printed in the United States of America
13 14 15 16 17   10 9 8 7 6 5 4 3 2 1

ISBN: 978-1-4675-6546-2

Dedication

I dedicate this book with joy to Georgia and Bill Johnston, my beloved mother and father.

Days after my birth in 1958, I was transplanted into their hearts and home through the gift of adoption. Over the years, they have nurtured me with the very best of themselves, and I've grown in strength and beauty because of it.

Thank you, Mom and Dad, for being the rich garden space I needed as a child to blossom into the person I am today. I know that I would not be in this place without your loving and supportive presence in my life. I'm like a tall, hardy sunflower with her face soaring skyward—ever blooming and growing in the light of God's love.

Contents

Foreword

The very first time I met Charlie, I was touched by his gentle, joyful presence.

When my husband and I arrived at the foster home where our newborn son had lived during his first month of life, we were welcomed warmly by his caretakers. Soon, a young girl appeared. Silently, she took my hand and led us down a long hallway to a sunny bedroom. Right away, our eyes settled on a bassinette with a sweet, rosy-cheeked baby inside. Our new son looked up at us, serene and smiling, as if to say, "I've been waiting for you—let's go home now!"

Charlie's serenity and joy have been a delightful addition to our family ever since that initial meeting in Oregon. From our first night together in a Medford hotel, life with him has unfolded with exquisite grace. Even as an infant, it was apparent Charlie had a joyful spirit. He was relaxed, unhurried and an easy companion.

Two decades later, his basic nature remains the same. Although he's able to voice his feelings and needs when necessary, he always finds his way back to his calm and gentle center. I've learned from living with Charlie that the heavier emotions are not to be avoided. Instead, they are to be wholeheartedly traversed in search of the peace and joy that live on the other side.

Many times it feels as though Charlie's the parent and I'm the child. Regardless of the circumstances, he's my carrier of strength and courage—always with the gentleness and understanding of one who truly sees. No matter what's happening with me, he's a fountain of life that never runs dry. My son is an angel of the earthly variety—of that, I have no doubt.

I knew when Charlie was just a small boy that his light would help show me the way. After twenty years as his mother, I still consider him my most trusted teacher. As I've stretched and grown over time, his lessons have become more advanced. My son challenges me each day, 'though unaware he's doing so, and I'm a better person because of it.

In this world where love without conditions can be a rare commodity, I'm grateful to be blessed with the chance to share my life with such a master. Under his tutelage, I, too, have become a bringer of hope and healing—and I've been taught by the very best.

With Charlie at my side, I'm shown a different way of seeing with every step.

Through his gentle, loving eyes, we're all "one people." He doesn't understand conflict, and he can't fathom barriers that push people apart. He doesn't know about ego and pride and the kind of fear that keeps love at bay.

This little book contains a homespun weave of vignettes from life with my very own angel. My wish is that you will find encouragement in these stories and a reminder of your own innate goodness. In the simplicity of Charlie's lessons, may you rediscover what you once knew as a child—that joy is your natural state and that all things are possible with love.

Jannirose JOY Fenimore

Introduction

I feel honored and humbled that Jannirose asked me to introduce her heart-filled book, *Loving Outside the Lines—Lessons from an Earth Angel.*

Our paths crossed 20 years ago after the birth of my first son, who was born with Down syndrome. The doctor's prognosis was grim as our newborn son experienced some medical challenges as well. After much heartbreak and agony, his father and I made the painful decision to give up this beautiful child for adoption. We knew we were unprepared and ill-equipped to provide him the best possible care over his lifetime.

Although Jannirose and I didn't meet in person at the time my son's adoption papers were being signed, I knew my precious little boy—who would soon be known as Charlie—was in the care of a generous, kind-hearted and loving woman. I already felt a deep sister-soul connection to her.

One of the biggest gifts Jannirose has given me is peace of mind and comfort in my heart about my decision. From the very beginning, I've known my son is in the perfect place for his special gifts to be recognized and lovingly nurtured. I'll always be grateful to Jannirose, her husband George and their son William for helping him to shine his brightest light.

The stories you'll read about Charlie and his natural ability to touch hearts are miracles to behold and savor. You'll see how he truly is a messenger of love, with his quiet invitation for us to expand beyond our perceived limitations. Most importantly, he gently encourages us home to our hearts.

My deepest admiration and blessings as you take this amazing journey with Charlie and his beautiful mom, Jannirose. May you be forever touched by these two earth angels, as I have.

With love,

Bronwyn Davis Marmo

Blessing

Bless this book about love and peaceful with loving and healing. It's a wonderful gift of joyful with holiness in our world to come in peace. The angels bring happiness to our spirits with their yellow lights and joy is to our souls with bright from the shining hearts.

CHARLIE FENIMORE

Charlie is Jannirose's elder son and her life's greatest teacher. He is an honorary peace minister, a Love Ambassador and a Special Olympian. He says, "I'm here with the angels to shine spiritness and happiness for loving everybody."

CHAPTER ONE

A Different Drummer

*"If a man does not keep pace with his companions,
perhaps it is because he hears a different drummer.
Let him step to the music which he hears,
however measured or far away."*

HENRY DAVID THOREAU

I've always marched to the beat of a distant drum.

Even as a child, I was tuned to an entirely different channel from most people. Because of this, making sense of the world was never easy for me—and still isn't. When I look back at my early years, I'm struck by the courage it took to express my authentic self. Especially during adolescence when there was such pressure to conform, I clung to the wisdom that whispered from the depths of my soul.

"This is who I am," it said, "and there's nothing I need to change."

By accepting the truth of that inner knowledge, I volunteered for a difficult ride through my formative years. But no matter how much grief I endured from others, I bravely pressed on—every step in time with the rhythm that flowed deep within me. Although there were days when I could barely make out the beat, I did my best to keep pace with the tune I heard inside.

My song, the one my Creator sang from the moment of my birth, the one only I could hear—the soothing notes that spoke my name as if it was the most beautiful sound in the world.

We all have such a song within us. It's the one we hear so clearly when we're young—the melody that invites us to bloom into full and glorious expression. It's the familiar tune that fades over the years as the world imposes its conditions upon us and we accept—unaware we might have another choice. As the years go by, it becomes harder to hear the song of our soul's deepest longing—the song that beckons us to a dance that is ours alone to dance.

To my delight in my teens, I discovered a group of people who seemed immune to the idea that they should change to meet other people's expectations. In these unselfconscious souls, I caught a glimpse of something familiar. Although I couldn't explain it, I felt I'd been reunited with beloved relatives from my distant past. What I loved most about these new friends was the integrity with which they lived. Because I'd noticed a lot of kids my age were afraid of being real, it was refreshing to find some who were so comfortable with themselves.

Through my initial encounter with these kindred spirits, I was shown what it meant to be truly free. I still recall the pure joy they showed at meeting me. Even though I was the new girl, I was embraced wholeheartedly from the start. In the company of such innocents, I felt fully accepted for perhaps the first time in my life. With these friends, I could be myself without concern that I would be judged or rejected.

That's how it happened when I began volunteering with Special Olympics. From my very first encounter with the athletes, I was welcomed as a cherished member of their family. On the surface, it probably appeared I was investing myself in a worthy cause, but deep down, I knew I was the one receiving the gift. It didn't take long for me to cultivate a real admiration for those who were perceived as "developmentally disabled." From these remarkable beings, I learned valuable lessons in living.

Is it just me, or does it seem wrong that people who are such experts at living in the heart are seen as "disabled"? Is it strange that they— who walk so gently on the earth, not trying to be anything but who God made them to be—are considered "handicapped"?

I soon recognized the irony of those labels. It seemed backwards to me that people who were so exquisitely honest in the way they lived—who lacked the capacity to judge others or see anything but beauty in their fellow human beings—could be seen as less than whole. Somewhere along the way, I realized we hold mirrors for one another as we journey through life. I've decided the images some folks reflect take an especially open heart to embrace.

Remember those magnifying mirrors from the carnival days of our youth—the ones that showed a person we didn't recognize as ourselves? "That can't be me," we'd think as we regarded the distorted picture in the glass. "It doesn't look like me at all," we'd say, staring at the unfamiliar image that loomed before us.

I suspect that's one of the invitations "differently -abled" people bring us in the unadorned living of their truth—they invite the rest of us to see ourselves with love and acceptance as we stand in the brilliance of their so-called imperfections.

———

I was fourteen years old when I received a message I interpreted as being from God. The words came through with such clarity that I had no question about the source of this special knowing: One day, I would have a baby with Down syndrome. I think that's why I was drawn to work with Special Olympians. On a level far beyond my awareness, I believe there was a place in me that knew what the future held.

Before I tell any more of my story, there's something I should explain. In case you don't know much about Down syndrome, it means the baby is born with an extra chromosome in every cell. In medical terms, it's called, "Trisomy-21," which indicates the presence of three chromosomes instead of the usual two on the twenty-first pair. In lay terms, chromosomes are the microscopic structures that contain the genetic information that determines the unique characteristics of an individual.

Normally, humans are born with twenty-three pairs of chromosomes, but every so often, something magical happens and another angel comes down to earth. Because of this extra chromosome, people with Down syndrome respond to the world a little differently from you and me. Unfortunately, it also means that most folks consider them to be deficient in some way.

At the first inklings of my Divine dispatch, I wasn't shown whether this child would come naturally or through adoption, but the details didn't seem to matter. Any way I looked at it, this was an unusual thing to hear, and I started to wonder if anyone would believe me if I tried to explain.

I mean, how many people would admit to receiving a message from God? Because I was at such a self-conscious age, part of me worried that if I talked about it, I'd end up looking crazy. Still, I felt excited about this mysterious message. I wanted to share my secret with the important people in my life, so I decided to take the chance. I'm not sure if anyone really thought I was crazy, but I soon discovered that not everybody sees Down syndrome as a blessing. In fact, I found that some consider it a curse.

"Don't even say that," one well-meaning person cautioned, "because it just might happen!"

After several attempts at sharing my joy, I finally stopped talking about it. I didn't appreciate the negativity around this personal glimpse into my future, so I became very protective of it. Eventually, I buried this precious knowledge in such a safe place inside me that it took almost twenty years to resurface into my consciousness.

Many years later as a young married woman, I suffered the heartache of a miscarriage. Still recovering from my loss, I lay down one day for a much-needed nap. When I woke up, I felt the familiar "knowing" from long ago that I would one day have a child with Down syndrome. This time it was revealed as much more than just a thought. I knew it was the truth.

I trusted this inner leading with my whole heart, so I walked into the living room to find my husband, George. Without hesitation, I asked, "What do you think about adopting a baby with Down syndrome?"

Even though it was an unusual question, I wasn't concerned about how he'd respond. My trust was so strong that it didn't occur to me to withhold it. Over the twelve-year span of our marriage, I'd never mentioned what I'd heard from God so many years ago because it had been hidden so deep within me.

Just as surely as I'd asked, George answered, "Why not? Let's do it!"

His words surprised me because of the importance of the subject. I guess I thought he'd need time to consider something as all-encompassing as adopting a child who'd be dependent on us for the rest of our lives. Hearing the certainty of my husband's response gave me the confirmation that something much bigger than we could understand was working in our lives.

Before Charlie was officially ours, I knew he had a special purpose in life. He'd be our first child, and we understood he was created with everything he'd need to live a good and fruitful life. Although much of the world tends to view Down syndrome as a genetic defect, we see it as beneficial to humankind. In our culture, where physical perfection and intellectual superiority are highly valued, people like Charlie are often seen as defective.

From the very beginning, we knew without question that he'd be every bit the reflection of God's love that we're each created to be. Once we made our initial decision to adopt, we received a lot of unsolicited feedback from people who questioned our choice to welcome such a child into our lives.

"You don't know what you're getting yourselves into!" some warned. "You'll regret it for the rest of your lives!" others threatened.

But through it all, we felt assured that our decision was right for us.

I remember filling out the paperwork required to be considered as adoptive parents for children born with Down syndrome. One section listed different characteristics we needed to choose to help us select our child, and that seemed strange.

Stop for a minute and imagine it: Choosing the attributes of a child based on personal preferences and assumptions of how those characteristics would fit into our lifestyle. It almost felt as though we were placing an order for a baby—something we weren't at all comfortable doing. The thought of selecting the race, sex, age and physical condition for our child seemed unthinkable.

As we scanned the various ethnicities and physical conditions, we realized we were ill-equipped to determine which qualities were acceptable and which were not. The only solution that seemed right was to check all the boxes and allow God to choose our baby, so that's exactly what we did.

The day we got the call about Charlie will be forever etched in our memories. We were living in Alaska and had been out enjoying a rare, sunny summer afternoon. When we returned home, the red light on the answering machine was blinking.

Feeling hopeful that it might be good news, I pressed the button to play the message and soon heard: "This is the Oregon Boys and Girls Aid Society. It looks like you're going to have a little baby boy in your home!"

In that instant, life changed for us. When we finally recovered from the shock of our happy news, we placed a breathless call to the social worker and began making plans to meet our new son. A few days later, we boarded a plane that would take us from Anchorage to the Pacific Northwest into the world of parenthood we'd dreamed about for so many long, childless years.

Life Is About Loving
by Charlie Fenimore

For us on this planet,
life is about loving.

Open our hearts about loving and feeling
and happiness and heartness.

The joy of sadness helps everyone heal.

Healing God and through the light makes
everybody's soul to be happy.

CHAPTER TWO

I Came to Heal Hearts

"Please God, make our hearts with open places
from joy for the world."
CHARLIE FENIMORE

One of the first things we learned about Charlie was that he'd been born with a small hole in his heart.

He had a few other cardiac issues as well—three separate valve problems to be exact—and the doctors told us he'd probably need surgery around the time he turned one. My natural response to this information was to lay him on my chest as often as I could while envisioning a golden light flowing from my own healthy heart to his. As I did this, I pictured that little hole being healed each day by the love that came through me from the heart of Creation.

It was during our little healing sessions that I started to see how Charlie and I were joined for a purpose that would later reveal itself. During those precious moments, I knew we were being knit together in spirit—this innocent baby that had grown in another woman's womb and myself, who had long yearned for the chance to have a child. From those intimate times of sharing between mother and son, I understood that God would use us to help open hearts.

Around Charlie's first birthday, his doctors released him from their care, telling us how they'd never seen such a dramatic case of healing without surgery. All I could do was smile and take joy in my private knowing that love is the greatest healing force in the world. Although the hole in Charlie's heart had diminished in size, we were told it would remain throughout his lifetime. Nonetheless, his medical team assured us that his quality of life would not be affected by this minute "open space" inside his heart.

Knowing him as I do now, the symbolism of his condition is crystal clear to me. He'll always have a hole in his heart, and it's from this place of openness and vulnerability that he lives.

~~~

Ever since he was very young, Charlie's had the emotional sensitivity of a wise, old soul. In fact, I'd call him a "spiritual savant," considering his keen ability to attune to matters of the heart. It might seem as though I'm saying this because I'm his mother, but in this case, it's the truth. Even in his first year, he'd sit in his high chair and observe us with rapt attention, gathering information to help him make sense of his world. It always amazed me to see this because of the intensity he showed as he watched the unfolding picture of our family life.

I remember a particularly difficult day a few years ago. In my memory, I'm lying on my bed, crying softly. Since Charlie has an uncanny way of tuning into my heart, I'm not surprised to hear his gentle knock on my door. I invite him in and through my tears, I see a look of genuine concern on his face as he walks toward me. Without words, he sits on the bed and snuggles in closely, his soft cheek against my wet face. Tenderly, he wraps his arms around me as the waves of sadness wash through my weary form.

As my son lovingly holds me, he slowly begins to speak: "For my sad Mom. We're going to pray for your heart. Please make this love shine bright to be your Godness."

I lie in silence and let the healing power of his intentions seep into my soul. As the tears dry and the balm of his words work their magic, he regards me deeply with a satisfied smile on his face.

"You happy now!" he proclaims.

There's a hint of mischief in his voice as he speaks. I'm not sure if he knows what he's done or if it's as mysterious to him as it is to me. All I know is that something's shifted inside me—something I can't quite identify—and it's as real as anything I've ever known.

"Yes, I'm happy now," I declare as convincingly as I can under the circumstances.

With delight, he lets loose the most glorious giggle, which dissolves the last remnants of my sadness. Then, we collapse together in a fit of laughter that transports me to a place of absolute joy. I can only imagine how comical we must appear—me with my tear-stained face and him with his wide-eyed expression—and the vision makes me laugh even harder.

As my emotions swing full circle, I point at him with a smile and say accusingly, "You really are an angel, aren't you?"

Unable to deny the truth, he admits with a sly grin, "Yes!"

Then I confront him with playful suspicion: "What are you doing here?"

At that, he simply answers, "Shining."

"So what are you shining?" I challenge—a bit perplexed by his answer.

"My heart," he says without apology.

"What makes your heart shine?" I say, pressing him for more information.

"Light," he says with an air of certainty.

To satisfy my curiosity, I take my questioning one step further. "What's the light for?" I ask.

"For God and for human beings." he says with complete authority. It's a strange and wonderful answer.

Once again, I feel something shift as I breathe the exquisiteness of this moment into my body.

"For God and for human beings," I repeat softly to myself.

Who in the world is this mystical boy, and what have I done to deserve him?

~~~

Whenever Charlie and I go through a trying time together, he hears a new prayer. This is what he does—it's who he is. It seems to begin like a tiny stream in the inner sanctum of his soul, rise into his heart and finally, emerge into the light of his awareness. When he asks me to get my notebook, I know he's about to bless me with the simple wisdom that flows so surely from the depths of his being. Sometimes, it's all he can do to contain himself until I'm ready to receive his gift.

"For my Mom," he begins, as if dictating a letter.

"This is all of the love.

This is of the spirit and the sadness.

This is true love and the One who loves them.

This is a part of life and the soul.

This is peace in the spirit.

Peace be with you, and I love you.

This is of the life and the peaceful.

This is a part of God and the power of love.

This is of the peaceful heart and the true love.

This is the spiritness, soulness, sadness, and gladness.

This is true of the heart."

After we sit for a while without speaking, he reaches over and takes my hand.

"I love it," I say to him in amazement. "I'm feeling much better now."

He answers me wordlessly with a big grin and dancing eyes.

It's times such as these when I remind myself to pay careful attention to this kid because he's here to teach me how to live.

~~~

We were driving home one evening after a sports awards assembly, and I was feeling downright fragile. A big part of Charlie's high school experience centers around what he calls "managing" the varsity teams. In reality, his title is almost entirely ceremonial, as there's little he can actually do on his own to assist the athletes and coaches.

The way I see it, he's the keeper of the team spirit, and his primary responsibility is to support his teammates with his whole heart and soul. In this respect, he's the best of the best. He wears a uniform, travels on the bus and sits with the guys on the bench during games. Although he's Bulldog Blue through and through, he lacks the necessary focus for any kind of independent supporting role. Nonetheless, in his mind, he's as much a part of the team as the starting players. And there's nothing anyone might say to convince him otherwise.

It's an exercise in trust for me to attend these sports banquets because a few times one of the coaches has inadvertently neglected to reward Charlie for his contributions. While I can understand these unintended oversights, it's painful to watch him standing happily with his teammates, expecting to get a letter or a medal like everyone else. But instead, he receives nothing to show for his efforts aside from a "thank you" from the coach.

Put yourself in my shoes: Watching your child go from proud and hopeful to crushed and dejected in a matter of seconds is almost more than any parent can be expected to endure. In my memory, the scene is still painfully clear. The awards have been handed out, and the closing remarks have been made.

When Charlie realizes he won't receive anything, he becomes very upset and rushes up to confront his unsuspecting coach.

"How 'bout me, how 'bout me!" he shouts to the bewildered man who can't fathom what my son's trying to say.

As students and parents file from the room, Charlie continues to plead his case.

"Make it happen for me! Make it right for me!" he shouts in desperation, as the popular coach begins to realize what's occurred.

With my heart breaking, I try to explain what's happening, but Charlie turns and runs for the door, shaking his fists in frustration. Following close behind, I reach out and grab his arm before he has a chance to leave the building.

As I look down at his troubled face, I see his eyes fill with tears.

Then I say to him gently, "It's all right to cry, honey."

Still fighting, he yells, "No, Mom, no! It's not right!"

I lead my precious boy away from the dwindling crowd and envelope him in my loving embrace.

"Let me hold you," I whisper as I pull him close to me.

Finally, he succumbs to his emotions and collapses into me, sobbing loudly. I cradle him for several minutes as he surrenders to the overwhelming anguish he feels from being forgotten once again. Sitting in reverent silence, I'm reminded of the breathtaking example my son brings to those of us who find it difficult to express our deepest pain.

I've always thought that when Charlie cries, he cries for humanity. I honestly believe our human family would be much healthier if we could summon the collective courage to face ourselves deeply with every step of the journey, as he does so well.

One of the beautiful things about Charlie is his willingness to embrace the entire range of his feelings. Even though there are moments when he tries to fight them, in the end, he knows what he must do. He's a stellar example for me of staying present through the peaks and valleys of life. As I watch the way he lives, I learn about what it takes to walk by faith in this uncertain world.

When Charlie's tears finally stop, he relaxes in my arms. With a sigh of relief, he lays his head against my chest as his breathing slows. After resting for a while in the stillness, he asks for some Kleenex. So I fish in my purse and produce a handful of tissues.

He blows his nose mightily and giggling, exclaims, "Man!"

Then he offers me a tissue and says in a concerned voice, "How 'bout you, Mom?"

It's his innocent way of saying he understands I'm hurting, too.

After I give my own nose a hearty blow, he says with admiration, "Nice one!"

"You were sad, too," he adds.

"We really got some feelings out, didn't we?" I say with a smile.

"Yeah, we did!" he answers, breaking into a wide grin.

As I wipe his tears, the light returns to his eyes.

"My face is pretty now," he says, still sniffling.

"Yes, your face is pretty with happiness," I assure him.

He stands up and proclaims with outstretched arms, "I'm better now. Let's go home!"

"O.K, let's go," I say, rising from the floor.

I take his hand, and we slowly walk out of the gymnasium, passing a few other parents along the way. From the expressions on their faces, I can tell they've witnessed our heart-wrenching scene and are deeply affected by it. As each one quietly acknowledges us, I sense the unspoken grief that we mothers and fathers share when our children hurt, and there's little we can do to ease their pain.

You know that feeling of powerlessness, even if you don't have kids. We all know it. It's the realization that nothing we might say or do can ever protect another person from experiencing life's hardships. In fact, we mustn't even try, for such is the sacred territory of the heartland. It's a journey the hurting one must make alone, as much as we would like to help them. It's the ultimate exercise in "Let go, let God," which always sounds so easy until it's staring us right in the face.

While Charlie's feeling good again and ready to leave, I'm still feeling sad. As he leads me to the parking lot, it's all I can do to put one foot in front of the other to simply walk. When we get to our car, I open the door and he climbs into the front passenger side. I buckle his seatbelt and instinctively place my hand over his heart.

"What you doing?" he asks.

"I'm praying for you." I explain.

"Your heart, too, Mom," he adds, "to help your confidence."

I think about this for a moment, and I have to agree with him.

"Thanks, I can always use more confidence," I admit.

Once I settle into the driver's seat, he leans toward me and places his small hand on my chest.

With great assurance, he speaks these words: "I'm healing you, Angel Mom."

When I can find the words, I softly say, "Yes, you really are."

When he tells me to get my notebook, I know he'll soon speak the prayer that I sense welling up from deep inside his soul.

"Write this,," he directs as I fumble to find a pen. "It's for their healing," he says.

He proceeds to mention the names of all of the people who witnessed his earlier pain: The coaches, the parents and the remaining students who were in the gym when he was overcome by crashing waves of emotion.

Then he continues:

"Their hearts about love of spirit and happiness
and the light for bright sun and angels.
This is love for all of them, for sad hearts.
The life and shining hearts of soul and
the rising world of the joyful.
Life is beautiful and wonderful
and the healing hearts is wonderness.
We must heal for somebody and everybody.
Love is about light and the planet of the sun.
From my soul of the sadness is the light of joyness."

So often, I'm left speechless after one of Charlie's special deliveries, and this time is no exception. When I finally start the car for the short drive home, I turn to him and smile. After driving a few blocks without speaking, he breaks the silence with the melody of his sweet voice.

"Mom!" he sings.

"Yes, Love Bud?" I say with deep affection for this angel who has come to earth disguised as my son.

With a tone of undeniable conviction in his voice, he declares, "I'm here to love everybody and help them with their happiness."

"That doesn't surprise me," I whisper.

Then he adds as an afterthought, "I'm a master of God and I came to heal hearts."

With the events of the evening still swirling in my mind, all I can do is gaze at him with admiration.

After pausing for a moment to consider the way he so naturally embraces his calling, I add, "I've been suspecting that for a long, long time."

~ ~ ~

Glory for Forgiveness
by Charlie Fenimore

*Brightness to our hearts and
to our soulness.*

*We have angels all around us and
the sun will shine.*

*Human souls on this planet are
glory for forgiveness.*

*The world is upon us to open our
hearts for healing love.*

CHAPTER THREE

Mitzi Was a Good Lady

*"We did love her heart and she had a great life. Her spirit
is wonderful and alive, and peace will make her home."*
CHARLIE FENIMORE

It was a "happy-sad" kind of day a few years back
when we were preparing to attend Mitzi's memorial service. I was happy because I'd had the chance
to know her and sad because I already missed her
like crazy.

Mitzi was one of the first friends we met after
we'd moved from Texas to Ohio, and for that reason,
she held a very special place in our lives.

You might know what it's like to pull up roots
from a community you really love and begin a new
life in a different place. It feels like a part of you is
dying, which is probably not too far from reality. It
can take time to heal from all that letting go.

This was the condition I was in when I met Mitzi, and I'll never forget the joy I felt in her presence. Charlie took an immediate liking to her as well. Because people aren't always sure how to act around him, we were delighted when Mitzi embraced him from the beginning with her whole heart.

Not long after we settled into our new home in Yellow Springs, I discovered a walking trail that meandered along the back edge of our property. I wondered where the path led and soon found it ended at a place called "Friends"—an eldercare community started by the local Quaker group. Normally, I walked alone with my dog, but this time, Charlie was with me. It was a cold winter morning, so I didn't expect we'd encounter another human being.

Picture it: A blustery winter day—snow swirling—the kind of conditions that would inspire you to hunker down before a crackling fire with a steaming cup of hot cocoa.

Struggling to stay upright against the wind, I'm shocked to see someone trudging through the snow in the distance.

"Wow," I think, feeling impressed. "These Ohio folks must come from sturdy stock."

As we close in on the small figure in the blue jacket, I realize this rugged soul is an elderly woman who's simply out on her morning stroll. Little do I know that we're about to meet Mitzi, who, I will soon learn, is cherished by most of the population of the village.

Then, she stops, looks directly at me and says, "Nice day, isn't it?"

But it's the twinkle in her eyes that captures my heart. I respond to her in a playful tone, "I'm surprised to find anyone else crazy enough to brave this bitter cold!"

A wide smile spreads across her wrinkled face. She extends one red-mittened hand and declares, "I'm Mitzi. You must be new in town."

Right away, I know I've found a kindred spirit.

You know how that feels. It's the sense you get when you find someone who seems really familiar, even though you've just met.

I'm impressed by how easily she relates to Charlie. After so many years of parenting my special boy,

I notice many people seem at a loss for words when they first meet him—but not Mitzi.

Respectfully, she steps back, studies him for a moment and nods her approval. "Who's this?" she asks with genuine enthusiasm.

As she gently takes his hands, my son proudly answers, "I'm Charlie Fenimore and I'm fifteen!"

The connection between the two of them is immediate and powerful, as if they've just been reunited after a long separation.

"Well, it's nice to meet you, Charlie." she says slowly. "I think we'll be good friends."

"Yes!" he answers, grinning broadly as he wraps her in an enthusiastic hug.

~~~

One of my best memories of our days with Mitzi comes from the time the three of us joined a group of amateur singers for a concert to honor the life and work of Dr. Martin Luther King, Jr.

The first thing I learned about our new friend was that she loved anything musical. I soon discovered she was the Minister of Music at her place of worship and owned a full-sized harp—something she decided to take up at the age of 60. When I found out about that harp, her coolness factor skyrocketed for me as I considered the freedom of spirit required to buy an instrument bigger than she was—and master it—all in the winter season of her life.

This little lady was fast becoming my hero.

I recall our initial rehearsal with the choir. We divide into groups according to our vocal range, and it turns out all of us are altos. As we take our assigned places and begin to sing, Mitzi seems perfectly at ease alongside Charlie—despite his inability to grasp the concept of reading music. I'm pleased at the way she regards him with such grace and understanding—accepting without judgment the miracle of his creation—not once trying to correct him.

Looking over at Charlie after we finish the first song, I savor his expression. He turns to Mitzi with an air of absolute wonder—mouth open wide in sheer delight—and she responds with a wise, knowing smile, squeezing his hand in assurance. There's an exquisite quality about our new friend that allows her to love with a wide-open heart, which is the same way Charlie lives.

A year and a half later, as Mitzi's time on earth is drawing to a close, my son regularly asks me, "Mitzi died?"

He has a strong sense that she will leave soon, and the simplicity of his question speaks volumes more than his words can convey.

"Not yet," I say, realizing he needs to talk about this special person who's come into his life.

During those last days, I tell him stories about our visits and how much she enjoys the friends who come to show their love for her.

When I finally receive the call that Mitzi had died, Charlie looks at me soberly and says with firm resolve, "Let's do a prayer."

That's my signal to find my notebook and join him on the couch to record his carefully chosen words. As we sit together in silence, he closes his eyes and listens deeply, waiting for the prayer to surface from deep inside his soul.

~~~

The memorial gathering for Mitzi is about to start, so we arrive early to find a seat. The room is already filled to near capacity with people of all ages who have come to celebrate the life of this remarkable lady who was so well loved. We find two empty chairs near the middle of the auditorium and settle in with the others to wait for the ceremony to begin.

Charlie's always been comfortable around the subject of death, an uncommon trait in our culture. I think his comfort relates to the fact that he's such a master in the art of loving.

In the company of the grieving, he sees only tender, open hearts.

He's one who truly lives to love, so whenever we have the chance to attend a memorial service, he's there—front and center, prayer in hand, ready to lavish his love upon those who are hurting. I've long understood these things about Charlie, but our new neighbors haven't had the chance to learn about his special gift.

As the memorial service begins, a recording of Mitzi's heavenly harp infuses the room, while images from her long life fill the screen before us.

"There's Mitzi," Charlie whispers with joy as the photo of a smiling young woman appears.

I watch as he studies her picture and savors the light that shines from her face.

He leans close to me, places his hand over my heart and asks, "You sad, Mom?"

My eyes meet his, and I answer weakly, "I'm happy-sad, Chaz."

In response, he lays his head on my shoulder and softly says, "I will heal your heart."

~~~

When the time comes for the sharing of memories by family and friends, Charlie is eager for his turn. It seems important to me that those who'd known Mitzi for many years should go first, so I hold him off as long as I can. But finally, when his patience runs out, he grabs my hand, pulls me to my feet and leads me to the front of the room.

As we wait for our chance to speak, we huddle close together on the stage, each with an arm around the other. I take the microphone first and tell a few of my favorite Mitzi stories as the crowd nods in agreement.

Soon, it's Charlie's chance to share his prayer, so I introduce him and sit down nearby as he prepares to speak. You might guess I'm a little nervous when I look out at the crowd of expectant faces. Since he's the only person with Down syndrome I've ever seen in our small village, I wonder how his simple message will be received. But I soon realize there's no need for me to worry.

As he stands at the podium, my son is met by over a hundred caring souls waiting patiently to hear his heartfelt words. With an angelic grin and the confidence of a seasoned speaker, Charlie squares his shoulders, takes a deep breath and prepares to talk about his beloved friend.

In a soft, measured voice, he slowly begins his prayer:

"Mitzi was a good lady.

We did love her heart and she had a great life.

Her spirit is wonderful and alive, and peace will make her home.

Her happiness is grateful, and her light is shining bright.

Her family and friends will miss her, but her spiritness is here.

Her peace is good for all of us and fills her heart with gladness.

It makes her spirit life, and her Godness makes us good."

Watching for the reaction of the crowd, I see smiles of appreciation spread from face to face as Charlie finishes blessing us with his words.

For that window in time, he's not a special education student or a developmentally-delayed teenager. He's not disabled in any way or mentally retarded or any of the other labels that society is so quick to place upon people like him.

Instead, he's a sensitive, eloquent young man who's doing his best to honor the memory of a dear friend who touched his heart. In this precious moment, we bear witness to a master teacher who shows us what it means to live without apology in the truth of his being.

When Charlie finishes speaking, he takes my hand and leads me back to our chairs. Once we're seated, he turns to me with the sweetest smile and whispers, "Nice!"

As his eyes sparkle brightly, he eagerly awaits my response. But all I can manage is a weak nod through my tears to affirm the beautiful gift he's just given with his whole heart.

After the service finishes and we stand to leave, I lose track of Charlie in the swell of the crowd. But I soon spot him standing near Mitzi's family, receiving people with hugs and loving pats on the shoulder.

As I observe from across the room, I feel I'm watching a wise, grandfatherly person instead of a seventeen-year-old boy. It's not only his gentle manner that impresses me, but the depth of his concern for these people he's never even met.

Standing back from this poignant scene, I'm struck by the ease with which he gazes so tenderly into the eyes of those who are feeling the loss of this dear lady.

It's times like these when I'm reminded of the treasures Charlie brings to my world. I discovered long ago that he holds little inside to prevent Divine love from infusing all that he says and does. He possesses a remarkable ability to stay in his heart through the daily happenings of life and because he does, he's ever ready to receive a full measure of God's grace.

As the crowd moves toward the foyer, Charlie makes his way back to me. Arm in arm, we're met by a long succession of people who want to thank him for sharing his heartfelt words about their beloved Mitzi.

In the purity of his simple prayer, he'd painted a glorious picture of this free-spirited woman who greeted each day with arms open wide. Through his keen perception, he recognized the joy with which she chose to live. As a sensitive soul, he was drawn to the way she treated people and the peace that colored her life.

When Charlie looked at Mitzi, I imagine he saw a clear reflection of his own gentle spirit. Although he'd miss her dearly, I believe he understood on a profound level that her essence would always remain, shining brightly through the hearts of those who loved her, making the world a better place simply because she'd lived.

Bright with Our Love
by Charlie Fenimore

Joy to the sky and the angels are there.

The sun shines and makes us bright.

With our love the people will be healed.

God tells us all to be in our hearts.

CHAPTER FOUR

People of the Joyness

"With our people of the joyness, we are not sad."
CHARLIE FENIMORE

There's something unmistakably beautiful about the way my son lives.

I'm continually impressed by Charlie's honest presence and gentle, loving nature. I can't help noticing the way he treats people with such pure love and respect. It doesn't seem to matter whether he's known them for a long time or has just met them. Either way, the connection he makes with everyone is always deep.

If you were raised in a religious or spiritual community, you were probably taught as a child that we must love each other. No matter which tradition you embraced, you likely came to believe that one of our most important responsibilities is to treat people as we would like to be treated. It's the Golden Rule we learn from the time we've barely started school. But as simple as it sounds, it's not always easy to live up to the challenge. So many things can get in the way of our ability to live and love from the heart.

One of my favorite qualities that Charlie and his developmental peers possess is their capacity to whole-heartedly accept strangers. Even when someone new joins their crowd, the person is immediately welcomed with big hugs and high fives. These joyful souls love so naturally, without conditions. I feel blessed to have someone to show me how it's done, every day of my life.

~~~

There was a time we went to a popular chain restaurant for a family dinner one Saturday evening and discovered there would be a long wait for a table. As we often do, Charlie and I stay to listen for our name to be called, while his dad and brother decide to pass the time in a nearby bookstore. There isn't much room in the crowded lobby, where a few dozen hungry patrons wait to be seated.

Charlie and I can find joy in even the most mundane situations. It's not so much about what we're doing, but the fun we have just being together. It's been this way from the time he was a little guy. Between the two of us, we've never had to work too hard at having a good time.

One of the things that tickles Charlie's funny bone is repeating the same word over and over again in rapid succession. I'm sure this sounds cute, but it can really make me crazy—and he knows it. As he does this, he breaks into his trademark angelic grin with glorious waves of laughter rolling through him.

With his face close to mine, he starts in a whispered voice, "I'm hungry, Mom!" And then the subtle assault begins.

"I'm hungry now, I'm hungry now, I'm hungry now, I'm hungry now, I'm hungry now!" he chants.

"I know, lovey. We don't have too much longer to wait," I say, hoping I can derail him before he drives me nuts.

"I wanna eat, I wanna eat, I wanna eat, I wanna eat, I wan-na eat!" he drones softly, dissolving into a fit of muted giggles as he tries hard to keep his rhythm.

As a defensive tactic, I do my best to ignore him.

"Mom! Feed me, feed me, feed me, feed me, feed me!" he chirps, sounding more like an obnoxious parrot than a teenage boy.

Then he moves closer, so we're almost eye-to-eye, and he waits for the telltale signs I'm about to crack.

"Stop!" I say with all the seriousness I can muster, "You're dri-ving me craz-y!" which delights him to the core.

"Food, food, food, food, foooood!" he quietly demands—laughing so hard he can barely speak.

"I'm starving, I'm starving, I'm starving, I'm starving, I'm starv-ing!" he pleads as convincingly as he can.

Charlie has the most contagious laugh, so it doesn't take long for me to be thoroughly infected by his happy spirit. Once I've surrendered to his joyous charms, he regards me with a satisfied expression—pleased that he's so expertly tickled my funny bone. I honestly think he feels responsible for opening hearts. It must be written somewhere in his job description.

When I finally collect myself, my eyes survey the crowd of people nearby—most of whom are texting or talking into their cell phones. It's strange to see folks together yet apart, sharing the same space but completely ignoring each other. This is the scene as we wait for our name to be called—with the exception of a small cluster of three.

Standing directly in front of us, the trio form a tight circle—facing inward, completely engaged in the intimacy of the moment. After studying them briefly, I gather they're a family: a mom and a dad and their beloved teenage daughter, who looks old enough to be in college. It's a wonder to witness their togetherness in the midst of such separation. In stark contrast to most of the people in the lobby, these folks are making eye contact—smiling and laughing easily—as they hug and hold hands in their private universe.

Charlie notices this right away and focuses his attention on these happy people with laser-like intensity. I can see he's being swept up in the surge of love they unselfconsciously project. It's the language of his deepest being, and he responds like a foreigner who delights in hearing his native tongue. As he takes in the scene before us, I watch the way he contemplates each face with the learned gaze of a master. He's transfixed by the sweetness he feels from this loving family. I can tell—I know the signs. Slowly, a smile spreads across his face and he shoots me a knowing look.

Nodding his head as if to agree, he carefully forms his words.

"Mom," he whispers.

"Yes?" I say.

"They have Down syndrome?" he asks with complete sincerity.

I pause for a moment before answering, "No, I think they're just happy."

Then, I consider the reason for his question and immediately, it becomes clear.

Recently, I'd challenged him playfully: "What are you guys with Down syndrome doing here?"

Without missing a beat, he said with certainty, "Spirit of joyness!"

In the simple act of family togetherness we were privileged to witness at the restaurant that day, Charlie saw joy. With his wide-open heart, he tapped into the happiness he clearly felt from these carefree strangers. Through the simplicity of his innocent deductions, he'd concluded the only thing that made sense from his experience: They must have Down syndrome because they were so genuinely, happily living their love.

~~~

During the decade we spent in southwest Texas, our school district held a yearly "Special Track and Field" event—patterned after the original Special Olympics. As much as I loved watching the children compete in their events, my favorite part of the games was always the open-air dance that was held at the end of the day. The dancing wasn't really a part of the competition, but a chance for everyone to celebrate in the joy of the gathering.

I still picture the athletes swaying to the music. They move with complete abandon, spirits as free as the desert wind.

"What a holy way to live," I think, and make a silent promise to always give my own spirit that kind of freedom.

With outstretched arms, dancers summon spectators to join in the fun. At first, it's clear that some of us are uncomfortable being in the spotlight. It shows in our body language and the self-consciousness with which we move. But soon, inhibitions fade and the spirit of love takes over. And for that brief moment in time, we're little children again as our joyful natures awaken from their lonely hiding places.

How many of us live from day to day, encumbered by concerns over what other people think? From the time we're kids, we receive messages from the world that we're not O.K., but something deep inside tells us to hold onto our individuality with all our strength.

As I savor the authentic way these special ones live, it occurs to me they must be untouched by the critical messages so many of us accept as truth. This is one of the gifts they so expertly bring: They invite us to remember the wonder and miracle of our creation.

~~~

I don't see my son as disabled, and he doesn't, either. From the very beginning of his life, I've considered him to be perfectly, beautifully Charlie. Sure, he does things in his own way and time, but there's nothing he's really missing. While he needs help doing certain things, he's quite capable in other ways.

At his first well-baby visit as an infant, we saw a new doctor who made it quite clear he disagreed with our choice to adopt Charlie.

I can still hear the harshness of his words echoing in my mind: "What are you thinking by taking on a child like this?" he spits out with disdain.

"He'll never go to college, and he'll be dependent on society for his entire life!" he challenges.

With a good measure of grace, I receive the perfect response: "I don't believe an advanced education or the ability to live independently are necessary for a worthwhile life," I counter.

"Charlie will spread love and joy in a way many people can't," I say with firm conviction.

Then I take a chance: "I've met a lot of folks who are successful by traditional standards but seem unable to live in their hearts."

I pause to get my bearings and then add: "Although my son may never earn a lot of money or hold a high-powered job, he'll make a loving investment in the lives of everyone who knows him—and that, I believe, will make a profound impact on the world."

When I finish my speech, the doctor looks at me a little sheepishly and says with a tight-lipped smile, "Congratulations on your baby and best of luck."

I was correct in my assertion so many years ago that Charlie's specialty lies in the realm of the heart. Time and again, the depth of his emotional understanding is revealed through the sensitivity he shows in his interactions with others. While he probably won't make the Fortune 500 list (neither did Mother Theresa,) there's a desperate need on this planet for people who are here for the sole purpose of loving and sharing joy.

God Shines Peaceful
by Charlie Fenimore

*People can change the world with
all of our souls to the light.*

*We have a good life for the hearts
and happiness of our spirits.*

*The angels are with us for the
shineness in our life.*

*Brightness hearts are healed and
God shines peaceful to our home.*

Chapter Five

One Hundred Angels

*"Spiritness of angels shining bright is
beautiful and wonderful and alive."*
Charlie Fenimore

Not long after he started sixth grade, Charlie needed a series of orthopedic procedures to correct a
congenital knee condition.

The first one was traumatic for him and its af-
ter-effects were uncomfortable and inconvenient.
But then we took him back for more. While surger-
ies are difficult for most people, they were terrifying
for Charlie because he couldn't understand why we
kept putting him through the same thing—over and
over again. I'm sure this felt like torture, and yet, he
was absolutely powerless to do anything else.

Ask any mom or dad whose young child has been hospitalized. Our kids look to us for protection—trusting we'll keep them safe from harm. But when they need surgery or other strange and scary things, we probably don't seem so trustworthy anymore. Especially for the littlest, it must be really confusing when we parents make them do all that frightening stuff.

Charlie was no different from any other kid in this respect. It still hurts to remember the way he looked at me with utter disbelief each time I forced him to undergo something painful, despite his tearful protests. His facial expression spoke volumes about the abandonment he felt each time I abdicated my role as his protector.

When I think of those days, I'm transported back to the fall of 2006 in southwest Texas. Charlie and I are making the three-hour trip from our home in Del Rio to San Antonio. He's quiet on the drive and seems rather introspective.

But as soon as I turn into the parking lot of the children's hospital, he starts to unravel. At this point, it doesn't matter what I say because he's completely surrendered to his emotions—he's unable to hear me from the depths of his private hell. Like a meteor blazing across the night sky, his fear roars mightily until it eventually burns out. The best I can do for my beloved son is sit with him in silence as he bravely traverses the territory of his hurting heart, alone.

In time, his initial wave of terror subsides, and he returns to calm. I get him in his wheelchair to begin the tedious process of checking in and being prepped for surgery. Back to his usual charming self, he touches the hearts of everyone he meets. It's as though he's the king and I'm his devoted attendant, caring for his every need. As he holds court from his mobile throne, I take the necessary steps to ensure His Royal Highness arrives at his destination by the appointed hour.

I have good reason to believe hospitals are one of the largest employers of angels this side of Heaven. From physicians to custodial crew, laboratory technicians to dietary aides, every person we encounter exudes a sincere quality of loving-kindness. As a parent, this is both a comfort and a blessing that softens the harsh realities of why we're here.

When Charlie and I finally roll into the pre-op holding area, he's assigned to a nurse who will prepare him for surgery. After a warm introduction, she hands me a hospital gown and sends us down the hall to a small changing room. As I close the door, Charlie makes it clear he has no interest in taking off his clothes. Adamantly refusing to follow instructions, he's unwilling to remove even his shoes. Once I realize he won't budge, I take him back to the nursing station to explain.

But instead of trying to force him out of his comfort zone, the woman gracefully accepts what Charlie needs to do.

Then, she shows us to a bed, but he refuses to get in it. He's unwavering in his attempts to maintain control, yet his choices are accepted with utmost respect. With everything else he's asked to do, he remains unmoved—but nothing is said by the nurses to try and change his mind. He doesn't take off his glasses when asked and declines the suggested pre-medication, yet through it all, the staff treats him with dignity. And although he remains mostly silent, they receive his message and do their best to honor it.

You might think I'd be upset in some way by my son's behavior, but really, I'm impressed by his strength of character—and I pause for a moment to consider it. Despite what's asked of him by the nurses, he's steadfast in honoring his deepest needs. For one so young, he's surprisingly mature in the way he willingly accepts himself. He excels at being fully present in his heart— even when it hurts.

As the time gets closer to surgery, an alternate plan is devised: I will change into scrubs so I can accompany my frightened son into the operating room. The surgeon comes out to see us, and stays with Charlie while I put on the gown, pants, bonnet and shoe covers. Once I'm ready, I return to find his doctor sitting on the edge of the bed—just two guys hanging out together, talking sports. This, I realize, will bolster Charlie's trust enough to submit to what's coming next.

Soon, we begin our somber pilgrimage to the O.R., winding our way through the inner sanctum of the hospital. Walking in silence, the surgeon leads the way with his precious cargo, carefully guiding Charlie's wheelchair through the maze of hallways. I fall in close behind, followed by the nurse who's been with us all morning. We pass several others clad from head to toe in scrubs, who nod with compassion at the sight of my son still fully dressed in his street clothes.

Not a word is spoken as we round the final corner and enter the brightly lit suite where the surgical team patiently awaits our arrival.

This is where it gets difficult for me as a parent.

The next wave of fear awakens in Charlie as we situate him alongside the gurney, so the anesthesiologist can begin sedation. The team has put off the surgery as long as they can—and now they must move forward. I'm instructed to restrain my son in a tight bear hug. As I do, a mask is placed over his mouth and nose to administer the gas that will put him to sleep.

Immediately, he begins to shout, "Mom! Stop! No!" and struggles with all his might to break free.

It's a difficult thing to do as a mother and goes against everything I believe in. A part of me needs to scream, too. Privately, I want to scoop Charlie into my arms and run far from this dreadful scene— away from all these horrible things. I want to hold him close and caress him and soothe his fears. But instead, I must submit to what's being asked of me.

All I can do now is whisper in his ear, "I love you"—over and over again until the anesthesia takes its full effect.

Once Charlie is unconscious, the nurses quickly dress him in a hospital gown. This is done with complete professionalism and kindness at the same time. It's unsettling to see my son in this condition, limp as a rag doll and so very vulnerable. But a part of me knows all is well, so I trust. With every ounce of strength I can summon, I kiss his head, express my gratitude to the surgical team and walk out the door. I'm careful not to look back as I place every ounce of faith I have in the One who's really running the show.

I find my way to the surgery waiting area and collapse into a chair, feeling like I've just been through the biggest test of my life. I breathe deeply, dropping into my tender heart to the feelings I'd earlier put on hold. And as much as I can, I rest and nurture myself until Charlie's out of surgery. Then I'm ready for the second round of the day's extreme mothering event—accompanying my child through a difficult experience with all the love my heart can hold.

This is how it goes each time we return for another procedure. Charlie fights the entire process, from the moment we arrive at the hospital to the last breath he takes before the anesthesia carries him away. When he opens to the full intensity of his feelings, any explanation or reassurance is wasted. He cannot hear from his faraway place, for he's completely immersed in the present. Charlie's always lived like this, and I've learned much from the way he stays so authentically in his heart.

The surgical plan calls for two extensive reconstructions to correct a knee cap that "floats" out of place—interspersed with several noninvasive procedures under full anesthesia to gradually straighten Charlie's leg. His doctors have high hopes he will one day walk with ease and comfort. But he doesn't understand any of this. All he knows is that every few weeks, I force him to undergo a truly terrifying experience.

When I think about that difficult year, I'm taken back in time to the final surgery in Charlie's long, grueling string of hospitalizations.

Once again, we make the early morning trip from our family ranch near the Texas-Mexico border. He seems thoughtful on the drive, so I'm careful to allow him the solitude he needs. His mood is much like an elite athlete preparing for a championship event—reaching deep inside to gather the power he'll need to push himself to greater heights.

As we turn off the freeway and onto the side streets, I hear Charlie say, "Mom."

I turn back to see his outstretched hand and take it in my own as I continue to drive.

"Pray," he says in earnest, so I do.

Feeling the energy of my intentions flowing to him, he responds with a knowing look.

Soon, we turn into the familiar parking lot, and he adds in a soft voice, "I have 100 angels."

Comforted by his revelation, I answer him with a smile.

Today, something seems different—his mood is uncharacteristically calm. When I announce that it's time to go, there's no protest.

Instead, he turns toward me and says with a look of wonder, "God bless the world, I love my life."

On hearing this, I'm rendered speechless and left to consider the shining example he brings to me. Charlie shows me how to live with nothing held back.

We go through our usual check-in routine and by now, the staff know Charlie and greet him by name.

Because he's such a social person, this delights him to the core.

Soon, we report to pre-op where we're directed to a cubicle to wait until it's time for his surgery.

But Charlie surprises the nurse by saying, "Gown, please."

With a look of deep respect, she hands him the garment. I take him to the changing room, where he willingly allows me to dress him in the hospital gown. We roll back to the bed with the nurses watching closely. They know Charlie's history and have lovingly supported him during the biggest challenges he's ever faced.

Something has changed in my son.

Independently, he asks for the pre-medication that will help relax him.

"Medicine, please," he says to the nurse.

I can tell he doesn't like it—it's given through the nose—but he takes it without protest.

He proceeds to take off his glasses, hands them to me and points to his feet. "Shoes," he says, so I lean over to remove them.

As I attend to his requests, I'm in awe of Charlie's maturity and trust. He's a completely different person this time—nothing like the kid who's been so defiant all along.

Soon, the surgeon arrives and is surprised to find him ready and waiting. Taking his usual place at the end of the bed, the man engages his patient in light conversation while I excuse myself to change into scrubs. Once I return, we begin the familiar trek to the surgical wing. As we negotiate the busy halls, Charlie allows his doctor to guide the wheelchair.

But as we get closer to the operating room, my son turns around and says, "Let me do it."

We watch with respect as he slowly rolls himself into the surgical suite. By now, the team is assembled—and witnessing the profound transformation of their young charge. Nothing is said as he painstakingly propels himself from the doorway to the gurney—one casted leg outstretched before him. Then his surgeon takes over and backs his chair into position.

As the anesthesiologist prepares to place the mask over Charlie's face, my son simply says, "Mask, please."

A deep stillness fills the room as the doctor hands the mask to his patient. Charlie takes it and bravely places it over his mouth and nose.

Then in a small voice, he says, "Hold me, please."

Of course, I oblige. "I can hold you, honey," I say with a tenderness mothers know so well.

As I gather him in my arms, he asks, "How 'bout everybody holds me?"

One by one, each person in the operating room comes to Charlie and soon, he's completely engulfed in a gentle sea of love. The scene is especially poignant because today, the surgical team is entirely male. With fourteen strong arms to hold us, Heaven and Earth meld into one precious heartbeat. In this sacred temple, my son is lifted on the wings of seven angels into God's loving hands where he will rest until their work is done. When he finally slips from consciousness, we are silent and unmoving for a while longer. Each in our own way, we are committing to memory this unexpected lesson in faith and the healing power of love.

Happy in Our Hearts
by Charlie Fenimore

God's light is for our happiness.

Forgiveness is healness for the world around us.

Make us to be thankful in joy and holiness.

When the sun shines in us we will be happy in our hearts.

Chapter Six

My True Self Is Light

*"My true self is light. It became to be
my normal life of the human being."*
CHARLIE FENIMORE

Charlie just shines.

He possesses the same luminous quality I've noticed in other kids born with Down syndrome. With his angelic countenance, he awakens something beautiful in people that seems to transport them back to their loving essence. This is something all children do, but for some unknown reason, those like Charlie retain this ability for a lifetime. My son is forever young, and his light still shines as brightly as the day we met him. Through his unassuming manner, he carries a golden invitation to love.

When he was just a few months old, his God-mother and I joined a loving spiritual community. During Sunday services, we sat near the main doors with our precious cargo tucked snugly into a baby carrier. People loved to caress his head as they entered the sanctuary, and it became a regular practice for some—as if he was a sort of touchstone that connected them with something larger than themselves.

Even the minister was not immune to Charlie's charms. At the end of each service, she'd pause at our row, lift him gently to her chest and cuddle him in her loving, grandmotherly manner. This little ritual became the exclamation point that marked the end of those inspiring meetings. We soon came to accept my son's unofficial role in the ceremony with a sense of gratitude for the goodness he evoked in people.

When Charlie was eight, we made a series of appointments for him at a busy clinic in a neighboring city. No matter what time we arrived on any given day, the waiting room was always crowded. But despite the large number of patients, there was never much interaction between them as they waited to see the doctor.

During one of our visits, I notice Charlie studying the scene with intense focus—gathering information through his finely tuned heart. Assessing the situation, he wastes no time getting to work. I observe from my chair as he approaches a large woman with a sad expression. As he innocently gazes at her, she lifts her head, meets his expectant eyes and slowly begins to smile.

"I'm watching a miracle here," I think to myself.

It always humbles me to see him in action because I'm allowed to share my world with such a gifted teacher. Life with him is like "Loving 101"— an in-depth study into the art of living love.

Satisfied by the woman's reaction, Charlie moves with purpose from one person to the next and works his magic. Through his gentle touch, he delivers a welcome reminder that we're never alone in this big wide world and that love is in constant supply when we're open to receive it.

I believe we're born with this knowledge, but often, the trials of life obscure what's true. When times get hard, it's easy to forget the things we know deep in our bones. The way I figure it, truth is standard equipment in the human animal, but remembering it's there in the midst of life's trials is an option we must choose—every step of the journey.

As Charlie moves through the crowd, there's a palpable change in the group's energy. People are talking now and laughing together and marveling at this little angel who's so intent on spreading joy. Watching him interact with these complete strangers, I'm given a real-time lesson in loving without limits.

Once he connects with almost everyone in the room, his last stop is an elderly gentleman who seems somewhere far away. Standing back, Charlie takes stock of the man and slowly leans closer to meet his tired gaze. Still, the gentleman does not respond. Patiently, my small son waits. Finally, Charlie reaches out and ever so gently, touches his knee.

In that moment, something breaks free inside the old man's heart. With arms outstretched and a joyous grin, Charlie grasps the large, shaking hands and pauses with reverence as a single tear rolls down the tired, wrinkled face.

Satisfied, my son looks at me as if to say, "See, Mom? This is how it's done."

~~~

Charlie was born with the ability to "see" with his heart.

Almost two decades later, he still views the world with that innate light-heartedness. I believe everyone has such capacity, but for many of us, it diminishes as the trials of life leave their heavy burdens upon our hearts. As I watch Charlie live, I notice there's not much to hinder the loving vision God gave him—his heart is truly light with love.

Except for the very young, I've met few people who are so naturally clear. I'll admit I'm not always there myself. As my inner journey takes me deeper by degrees, I'm remembering what I once knew as a child. Those of us who travel the inward path must continually transcend the barriers that keep us from loving without conditions. For many of us, it's a life-long endeavor—if we're honest about it. But I also have a feeling it's the most important key to our spiritual freedom.

~~~

Charlie is our family's "E-ticket." If you've ever been to Disneyland, you know that's what gets you onto the most amazing rides. We found out long ago that having him in our lives has the same benefits. Normal occurrences turn into special events when he's with us, and I think it's because of the way he shines—his light precedes him everywhere he goes. For those who can really see Charlie, he's a shining beacon that calls them home to their hearts, and from that place of wholeness, love flows with blessed abandon.

There's a time I remember from Charlie's middle school days: It's the night before I'm scheduled to give a presentation to a large group of people. Because I'm planning to speak about the lessons I learn from my son, it makes sense that he'll be there with me. And because Charlie's such a giving person, he decides he wants to bring presents for everybody— all 100 people.

Even though I have much to do, I can't say no to his generous streak—so I get creative. I do a quick inventory of my craft supplies and soon find my solution: A large sack of round, flat river stones and a big jar of gold paint. Soon, Charlie's busy painting lopsided golden hearts on the entire bag of rocks. Hearts are something he can do and he loves to make them. When he's finished, he places his masterpieces one by one on cookie sheets, where they'll dry during the night.

The next day, the talk goes well. People seem genuinely inspired by my message and they're delighted to meet my son. As the applause fades, Charlie begins to hand out the rocks he so lovingly decorated the previous night. I watch with pride as he places a smooth stone in each waiting hand. He takes time to connect deeply as he slowly moves from person to person. No one leaves his or her seat as our love ambassador makes his rounds. Instead, they wait in unhurried silence for Charlie's humble gift.

There's a feeling of reverence in the conference room as a small blond angel blesses 100 hearts. While those in attendance may forget my talk, I have a feeling they'll remember the day their lives were made brighter by the light of a young boy's love.

⌒⌣⌒

Generosity is a strong thread in the fabric of Charlie's world.

Early in his life, he designated himself "Official Giver of Gifts", a title he still bears proudly in our family. The part he seems to most enjoy about his coveted role is the touching of hearts. Whenever a gifting opportunity arises within our circles, Charlie assumes he'll be the one to deliver the goods, and will defend his position mightily if challenged.

I have countless stories about his affinity for surprising the people he loves with gifts.

One particular story stands out in my memory because of the powerful lesson I was given in the true meaning of unconditional love.

It's December of his fifth-grade year—a day before the start of his two-week winter break. Charlie and I have presents for his teachers, aides, and everyone else who helps him at school. We put a lot of thought into selecting special gifts and had a good time wrapping them in festive paper and ribbons. Before leaving home that morning, Charlie affixes the bows, while I place each of the few dozen items in its own small bag.

Once we arrive at the school, he insists on carrying as many of the little bags as he can hold. "I do it!" he says as I fill his hands.

"I do it!" he repeats, a little louder in case I didn't hear him the first time.

Smiling broadly, Charlie struggles not to drop his precious bounty as we follow the walkway that leads to the main entrance. I'm feeling happy, too, as I consider all the beautiful people who helped him this year and imagine giving them each a small token of appreciation.

Loaded with treasures, we approach the double doors to the building. While I plan our delivery route, Charlie spies an elderly couple ahead. They move purposefully, with the tired but satisfied look of grandparents caring for their children's kids. Before I can stop him, he rushes toward the man and woman. As they notice this little stranger galloping wildly in their direction, they take in the picture with amusement. They don't know Charlie, but they've likely seen him around the school. With joy, he presents each one with a colorfully wrapped present that they accept with genuine sincerity. He then stretches out his short arms and they respond by surrounding him in a warm embrace.

While I process this joyous scene, it occurs to me that two of the people on our list won't receive anything from us. So I begin to mentally rearrange my busy day to include shopping for replacements.

As I'm deep in thought, Charlie's deep in his heart—and now barreling toward a young mother with two toddlers. Soon, he's handing each of them a present as well. The woman smiles and the children dance with joy as my son simply beams. He turns to me with the brightest of smiles and proudly nods his head. In Charlie's eyes, he's done something that deserves great praise, and he's not shy about telling me.

Shaking him from his reverie is the sight of a deliveryman—his next target. He makes a beeline for the unsuspecting man who is carefully guiding a loaded cart through the entryway and thrusts one of the little bags at him. Surprised, the tall man leans down to Charlie's level and speaks to him softly. My son answers by hugging the long, uniformed legs before turning to run back to me. The deliveryman stands motionless as he watches his secret Santa from across the room. As the man holds the brightly wrapped package in one hand, he waves at us, with a look of wonder on his face.

This pattern continues as Charlie makes a mighty effort to distribute all of our presents. Before he's finished, he's surprised the custodian, two of the lunch ladies, a few kindergarten students, some parents and the school secretary—giving each one a special gift. One by one, they're tickled to receive a present from my enthusiastic elf.

I watch with misty eyes as Charlie singlehandedly spreads a wave of Christmas cheer throughout the lobby—igniting many hearts in the process. And this is how it goes, until every single package finds a home. While I know I'll have to invest more hours shopping, wrapping, and delivering, the light shining in his eyes is worth far more than the extra time, effort, and money it will cost to replace the gifts he's so lovingly dispersed.

You might wonder why I didn't stop my son from his random acts of giving that morning.

As a parent, I've learned there are times for setting limits and times for allowing unexpected miracles to happen. This was one of those miracle moments. Charlie's actions that day were the most stunning displays of unconditional love I'd ever seen. I was so concerned about getting the gifts to the right people—to thank them for their contributions to his life—that I lost track of what it means to share freely from the heart.

But on that cold December morning, a real-live angel showed me how true love has no bounds and joy is the best reason to give.

Joyful To Our World
by Charlie Fenimore

*Spiritness from God and the angels shining
bright from happiness.*

*The soul of joy and light is feeling hearts
to be made with love.*

*We are thankful for joyness and sadness to
open our hearts with living light.*

*Shining bright with graceful giving joyful to our
beautiful world.*

CHAPTER SEVEN

Kind Is Our Relationship

*"Spiritness is kindness—everyone must make this under-
standing. Kind is our relationship."*
CHARLIE FENIMORE

As Charlie's mother, I'm given everyday lessons in the art of kindness and a reminder of the most important things in life.

I watch how Charlie so naturally treats people, and it makes me realize we could use a lot more "kind" in our dealings with one another. I'm not sure whether we're uncomfortable with deep connections or if it's something else that keeps us from loving well. One thing I've learned from my son is that a pure heart is the main ingredient in the making of strong relationships. Because he stays clear, he's able to reach those who are open to receiving his special brand of kindness.

Charlie loves it when visitors come to our house. Because his bedroom is on the main level, he's put himself in charge of answering the door. He feels so strongly about this responsibility that he won't allow anyone else to do it.

"I'm the doorman," he says proudly, "I let people in."

The first time I heard this, I had to pause to consider the deeper meaning of his words. And soon, I realized how much truth was in his innocent statement: Charlie's an expert at inviting people into his heart—with him, it's a door that's always open.

One of the sweet things about Charlie is the way he responds to human interest stories in the news. Especially when the stories are tragic, he reacts with sincere compassion and concern. He wants to know all the details—and gets upset when we can't provide them. Even when he doesn't know the people involved, his heart is touched as if they were his own.

Since Charlie was a little boy, he's had a profound awareness of other people's needs. So many times he'd witness suffering and vehemently demand that I help. No matter what I was doing, he'd expect me to drop everything and tend to the one who was hurting. And even as a young adult, he continues to hold me to his uncompromisingly high standards.

There are times when it doesn't seem appropriate for me to step into a situation involving other people, but still, Charlie expects me to do something.

"Mom!" he says when he sees a crying child with his mother. "Help him!"

When I try to explain why it's best for me to stay out of other peoples' business, he won't listen. He never does.

In his eyes, it must appear as though I've really missed the point. He gets seriously disappointed when I fail to meet his stringent expectations for loving service.

He won't even look at me at those times. Instead, he just turns away, indignantly.

But soon, he's back to his old light-hearted self and will once again accept me with all my human limitations.

~~~

I recall a family vacation a few years ago to Washington, D.C.

While my husband and other son prepare to leave for a tour of the Capitol building, Charlie and I decide to explore the neighborhood near our hotel:

It's a cold and blustery day, and people are bundled warmly against the wind. Just ahead, we notice a homeless man who's clearly in need—poorly dressed for the frigid temperatures.

In typical Charlie style, he takes my hand and pulls me into a coffee shop, where he tells me to buy a "really big hot chocolate." Then he notices some foil-wrapped candy hearts, and he points to them.

"He needs those hearts," he says with urgency.

I scoop up a handful, but he shakes his head and says, "More, Mom."

So I grab as many as I can hold, and he says, "Good job," beaming brightly.

He insists on holding the cup and the bag as we leave the store and soon, we're approaching the thin, scruffy man. Charlie walks up to him wearing his most angelic expression and extends the hot steaming cocoa to his new friend.

Tentatively, the man takes the cup into his gloveless hands and with eyes closed, takes a long, satisfied drink.

Silent for a moment, he then speaks. "That's the best thing I've tasted in a long time," he says, now looking at us gratefully.

As often happens in my life with Charlie, a beautiful lesson is taking form before my eyes. So I watch carefully and learn from the way he lives. My son says nothing, but his smile speaks loudly.

Then he lovingly places the sweets into the calloused hands and stands back, waiting for a reaction. As the man peeks into the little sack, a grin slowly spreads across his bearded face. He appears thoughtful for a moment, as if recalling a faded memory from happier days.

"Thanks, little guy," he says, extending his free hand toward Charlie.

"Yeah," says my son, nodding as he shakes the man's hand.

As we turn to walk away, the man adds with a note of wistfulness in his raspy voice, "It's been a long time since somebody gave me a Valentine."

Living with Charlie is a little like having our own resident Yoda in the house. He maintains a mostly silent, solitary presence and continually radiates light and love. When the occasion presents itself, he blesses us with his simple wisdom. He keeps a watchful eye on our family happenings—it's akin to having a lifeguard on duty 24/7. He has his fingers on the pulse of our collective heart and, in his own endearing way, administers loving aid when needed.

Charlie says he has "thousands of angels," and I believe him. We are so fortunate to be watched over by him and his angelic team.

Like any other family, we sometimes have what a minister friend calls "aggressive fellowship." When these rough patches arise, we all have a chance to heal and grow together.

These are the times when Charlie's gifts shine the brightest. Or maybe it just seems that way because the contrast is so great.

In the midst of such turbulent moments, Charlie shifts his loving into higher gear. He comes into the room where conflict is erupting and holds a quiet vigil. He stays in the background, saying nothing, and simply stands watch. That's his way of helping, and it's done entirely without words.

One particular evening, he leaves his post to get ready for bed. I think he's decided he's done all he can for us, and it's time to rest.

A few minutes pass, and then we hear his soft voice saying, "Good night." In unison, we turn toward Charlie just in time to watch him walk into his bedroom. We are stunned to see the shirt he's chosen to wear to bed—he calls them "sleeping shirts" since they're reserved for nighttime only.

Just before he closes his door, we catch a glimpse of Dr. Martin Luther King's poignant words printed on the back of his shirt: "We must learn to live together as brothers and sisters or perish together as fools."

As we allow the power of the message to take hold in our hearts, we look at each other with wonderment. I'm not sure Charlie does this consciously, but on a deeper level, I think he knows he's an instrument of Spirit sent to awaken us to the truth.

～ ～～

Charlie's always been a family guy. And as he's gotten older, his definition of family has expanded with each passing year. Now, it's grown to the point where everyone who's kind to him is considered kin.

He's especially interested in connections between people and can talk tirelessly about who's related to whom. When someone new comes into my life, he inevitably peppers me with questions about their lineage.

"He has a sister? He has a brother?" he'll ask, trying to piece the puzzle together.

"He has a daughter? He has a son?" he persists, then adds, "He has a mom and a dad?"

Charlie can get pretty frustrated when I'm unable to provide him with the answers he seeks because he has such a strong desire to know about people.

Not long after we moved to Ohio, an intense storm hit our village, and we were without power for days. The schools were closed, so we camped in the basement with a lantern and had good old-fashioned, human-powered fun.

Once electricity was restored, the kids returned to school and were asked to write an essay about the storm. Charlie wrote an entire handwritten page, which probably took him the better part of an hour to complete:

"The Big Storm" by Charlie Fenimore

We had a big storm and I stayed home with my mother and brother. My father was at work in Texas. He flies airplanes in the Air Force. I have Grandma Georgia and Granddad Bill and Granddad George and my Sky Grandma and Uncle Gary and Aunt Lindsey and Aunt Mern and cousin Jenna and cousin Meagan and cousin Lauren and cousin Ben and Uncle Art and Aunt Wendy and cousin Jeff and cousin Kim and Uncle Allen and Aunt Elaine and Uncle Rob and Aunt Anne and my birth family and Miss Mary and my friends Dominik and Ramon and John and Rolando and Karson and Oscar and Mike and Jay and Tyler and Travis and Hunter and other Tyler and my dogs Redford and Sadie and my cats Jeffrey and Jasmine and everybody who loves me and I love them all.

It was interesting to me, but not at all surprising, that the biggest part of Charlie's essay was about the people he loved.

Instead of focusing on his outer experience of the storm, he turned inward to thoughts of those who were most important to him. While the powerful storm swept through our neighborhood with great intensity, it carried Charlie to a gentle place within—a place where love resides in constant supply in the memories of the very special people who have graced his world.

~᠊ᐤᐧᐤ᠊〜

Angel's Love
by Charlie Fenimore

To glory for the planet and all the people.

Our happiness from the hearts of the human body.

This is for our world to be healed in light.

Kindness and shining stars of spiritness make our hearts with angel's love.

Afterword

Living with Charlie teaches me about the everyday miracles that are born when we embrace life in the spirit of love.

In this human experience, I believe our natural state is oneness with the Divine, ourselves, our brothers and sisters, and all expressions of life. This is our birthright and our essence. But somewhere along the way, we learn to build inner walls that keep us feeling separate and alone in the world.

I believe with all my heart that humanity has so much more potential than that. We've entered a time when people around the globe are awakening to the possibility that we may need one another far more than we could have ever imagined.

My own journey reinforces this idea with each new day.

When I consider my prayer for my future, I'd have to say I want to be like Charlie when I grow up. I hope to see as he sees—no longer a hostage to my misguided perceptions. I need to be pure in heart without the pain I've harbored deep within. More than anything else, I wish to love as he does—outside the invisible lines drawn by my deepest fears—free to embrace the world as the unique and beautiful person I was born to be.

If that's what it means to be disabled, count me in.

Acknowledgements

I realize that my story is the collaborative effort of many wonderful people.

First, I am grateful to my Creator for singing me into existence with such JOY—and to my birth parents for being my passport to the world.

To my Mom and Dad: You are the wings that help me fly.

To my husband, George: Your generous, supportive ways make it possible for me to freely explore the leadings of my spirit.

To my son William: Your innate creativity inspires me to envision the untapped potential that awaits my discovery deep within.

To my sister Wendy: Your belief in me from the time we were small teaches me to believe in myself.

To my brother Allen: Your steadfast, loving presence and your willingness to hear my stories throughout the entire creative process are the rarest of treasures.

To my sister friend Cara: Your talent and experience as a writer invites me to consider that I, too, can touch the world with my message.

To my angel friend Lisbeth: Your natural healing abilities free me from the limitations of my past and allow me to embrace the magic of each moment.

To my dear friends: Your love lifts me high so I can better see who I am.

To my friend and mentor Jimmy James Twyman: Your recognition of the power of Charlie's prayers and your skillful coaching breathe life into my storyteller's heart.

To Christy Collins: Your patient guidance through the publishing process is a comfort, and your design sense makes my story come alive.

To Gaelyn Larrick: Your receptivity to the magic and mystery of Source gives soul to the cover art for this very special book.

To Andrea Chapelo: Your sweet personality and exquisite way of seeing captures Charlie's angelic persona on camera.

To Ellen Dawson-Witt: Your keen editing eye brings greater clarity to my writing.

To the people of Del Rio, Texas: Your celebration of Charlie and your kindness to my entire family during our Lone Star years shine through the pages of this book.

To the people of Yellow Springs, Ohio: Your strong sense of community creates the fertile field I need to bloom and grow in the heartland.

To Charlie's birth parents: Your ultimate gift of a beautiful baby boy is a blessing that will last forever.

To my son Charlie: Your innocent lessons in loving remind me to always live from my heart.

About the Author

Jannirose JOY Fenimore is a Spirit-led weaver of words whose poignant stories awaken souls and inspire hope in the hearts of readers of all faiths.

A peace minister and master teacher and practitioner of natural therapies, Jannirose believes her life's greatest work is to assist her son Charlie in giving his message wings to fly.

Charlie—whom she calls her "earth angel"—says her job in this lifetime is: "Healing for humankind to be lightful for living in Heaven on Earth." Jannirose hopes to do her small part in fulfilling her son's lofty vision, every step of her journey.

A native Californian, she lives with her family in the colorful little village of Yellow Springs, OH and looks forward to one day returning to their ranch near Mt. Shasta, CA.

Invitation from Charlie

Come see my own book about life and love and shining spirits. It is called **Happy in Soul— A Very Special Prayer for Peace.** *We made it from my words with peaceful heartness and pictures of loving people.*

I have a Facebook [page] where you can be my friend and it is called "Lessons From an Earth Angel." My mom writes some stories there about our life, and I do my prayers to give hope for healing brightness.

Love, Charlie Fenimore

To learn more about Jannirose and Charlie's work, or for books and angel cards, please visit their websites:

www.JanniroseJOY.com
www.LovingOutsideTheLines.com
www.LessonsFromAnEarthAngel.com
www.HappyInSoul.com

All products are available for purchase on Amazon.com.

Holiness is for
everybody
and someone.

CHARLIE FENIMORE, *HAPPY IN SOUL*

Bless our hearts and the
wonderful spirits of angels
shining bright
with happiness.

Love from your friend, Charlie